1000 Years of Scottish Churches
Churches from before the Reformation to 1700

John R. Hume

St Serf's Parish Church, Dunning

© John R. Hume, 2018
First published in the United Kingdom, 2018,
by Stenlake Publishing Ltd.
www.stenlake.co.uk
ISBN 978-1-84033-762-4

The publishers regret that they cannot supply
copies of any pictures featured in this book.

Printed by
Berforts, 17 Burgess Road, Hastings, TN35 4NR

Dedication

To everyone who has been responsible for the creation and maintenance of church buildings in Scotland over the last 1000 years

Acknowledgements

My prime acknowledgement is to my family, my wife Hope and my sons Matthew, Kenneth, Peter and Colin for their support over many years, and my father William Hume who introduced me to churches of a wide variety of denominations: without them this series of books could not have been written

Over a lifetime of involvement with church buildings I have cause to thank the many people who have given me insights both into individual congregations and into church organisation. I am particularly grateful to the Church of Scotland for periods of service as an Advisory Member of the General Trustees and as a member of the Committee on Artistic Matters (now the Committee on Church Art and Architecture). While I worked with what is now Historic Environment Scotland as an Inspector of Ancient Monuments, and subsequently as an Inspector of Historic Buildings I had opportunities to visit many of the buildings included here. I am also very grateful to the staff of Historic Environment Scotland, and particularly Veronica Fraser, for supplying me with digital copies of some of my photographs.

As a founder member of Scotland's Churches Scheme and as a Trustee both of that body and of its successor, the Scotland's Churches Trust, I have developed a knowledge of the church estate throughout Scotland which in a very direct way prepared the way for putting together this series. I am most grateful to my colleagues on both bodies.

It would be invidious to single out a few of the many individuals who have helped, but I feel that I must mention the late Frank Lawrie, my superior officer in Historic Scotland, who was very supportive of my work with churches. I would also like to thank Stenlake Publishing for undertaking the publication of this series, and the staff of the Mitchell Library, Glasgow for their assistance over the years.

Finally, I hope that my many friends in church and architectural circles will realise that they are all included in these expressions of gratitude.

Further Reading

There are many histories of individual churches in Scotland, variable in quality, but none negligible. Most of them concentrate, understandably, on congregational life, and often say very little about church buildings, but all are worth reading to build up a rounded history of the Church in Scotland. In the preparation of this series of volumes I have found the following more comprehensive books particularly useful:

Ewing, The Rev W, *Annals of the Free Church of Scotland*, T and T Clark, Edinburgh, 1914

Groome, FH (ed), *An Ordnance Gazetteer of Scotland*, 2nd edn, William Mackenzie, Edinburgh and London, c1895

Hay, G, *The Architecture of Scottish Post-Reformation Churches, 1560-1843*, Oxford University Press, 1957

Hume, JR, *Scotland's Best Churches*, Edinburgh University Press, 2005

Lamb, The Rev JA (ed) and Macdonald, *The Rev FAJ (ed), Fasti Ecclesiae Scotticanae: Ministers of the Church of Scotland, vols I-XI*, various publishers and dates

Lamb, The Rev JA (ed), *The Fasti of the United Free Church of Scotland, 1900-1929*, Oliver and Boyd, Edinburgh, 1956

Small, The Rev R, *Congregations of the United Presbyterian Church, 1733-1900*, David M Small, Edinburgh, 1904

Various authors and publishers, *The Buildings of Scotland* and The Royal Incorporation of Architects in Scotland *Architectural Guides* series.

Also the Sacred Scotland series of handbooks and other publications of the Scotland's Churches Scheme and the Scotland's Churches Trust.

Series Introduction

The oldest churches in Scotland for which we have firm above-ground evidence appear to date from the early-mid-11th century. Before that, however, there were probably wooden churches, as found in excavations at Whithorn. There are also the round towers at Brechin, Abernethy and Egilsay which may be earlier than the earliest surviving parts of stone churches. The establishment of focal points for Christian worship probably pre-dates the construction of church buildings, and many of the surviving free-standing sculptured crosses may have been intended for that purpose. Good examples of such crosses can be seen at Aberlemno, Glamis and Logierait in southern Pictland, and at Nigg, Shandwick and Hilton of Cadboll in northern Pictland. In what was Gaelic Scotland there are fine crosses at Kildalton, Islay and on Iona, while in the cradle of Christianity in Wigtownshire there are crosses in the Whithorn Museum and in the parish church of Kirkinner which probably fulfilled a similar role. This practice of marking 'sacred places' with stone monuments can probably be traced back from early Christianity into the Bronze Age and the Neolithic period.

The purpose of this series of volumes is not, however, to engage in debate, scholarly or otherwise, so it is fair to assume that the earliest roofed stone Christian churches are about a thousand years old. In the lecture I gave in 2014 for the Scotland's Churches Trust, I showed photographs of about 100 churches from the 11th to the 21st centuries, mostly existing buildings, but including some demolished during the past half-century or so. In preparing this series I have drawn on the material collected for that lecture, but have supplemented it by including many more churches which shed light, for one reason or another, on changes in church organisation, worship practice and architectural fashion over the millennium concerned. The original choice of buildings was explicitly personal: churches with a particular meaning for me by virtue of aesthetic appeal or association, or both. I have carried this through into the present collection, which also takes account of geographical and denominational diversity. This will, I hope, not be considered egotism: it is just that I believe that I cannot write honourably or convincingly in this context about buildings that do not have some real meaning for me. A handful, however, have been included because they 'ought' to be there; I will not identify them. A few years ago I wrote a book entitled *Scotland's Best Churches*, which concentrated on churches then in use. Here I have included churches not in use as such, roofless and ruined buildings, parts of buildings, and some now demolished. I have endeavoured to present a balanced selection of churches of different periods, denominations and architectural styles. In captioning I have concentrated on highlighting particular points of interest relating to the images, rather than giving 'potted histories' of the buildings concerned. The number of changes in the names of churches over the years has made it impossible to include them all; in a few instances I have included more than one. As far as possible the first name quoted is the original one. The assigning of dates is very difficult. I have chosen to list churches by date of completion rather than date of design or commencement of construction. I have used my judgement in interpreting the various dates to be found in published sources. Because old counties were an important context for church building I have used them in headings; modern local authority areas are not notably helpful.

Finally, please do not look on this collection as a work of scholarship (though I have done my best to make it scholarly). Look on it, rather, as a love-letter to the Church Universal. Each of these buildings is in its own way a place to encounter God, Father, Son and Holy Spirit, and to go out into the world imbued with the idea of loving God and loving our neighbours.

John R Hume
Glasgow
March 2018

Sustaining Scotland's places of worship.
15 North Bank Street, Edinburgh, EH1 2LP
0131 225 8644
Registered Charity: SC043105

Churches in Scotland before 1700

My understanding of the background to the construction of the oldest surviving stone church buildings was outlined in the Introduction. Churches as we know them were, however, first built as an outcome of the introduction of feudalism into Scotland in the late 11th and early 12th century, to replace earlier tribal patterns of land-ownership and allegiance. In the feudal system all land was the property of the monarch, and its administration was delegated to 'nobles'. In the parts of Scotland where feudalism was implemented the land was divided into 'baronies' which by and large were also designated as parishes. From the later 11th century abbeys and priories were established, at first by the monarch, and later by noble families. The abbeys were large and powerful establishments, and to support them the revenues of large numbers of parishes were allocated to them. The wealth of these institutions was largely created by the sale of wool shorn from sheep grazing on the monastic parishes. It was at this time that the first parish churches were built, some of which are included in this selection, as are some of the great abbey churches. The oldest of these buildings were in Romanesque style, with round-headed windows and doorways. Some have or had semi-circular apses at their east ends. This feature appears to be characteristic of areas in western Europe where Norse influence was strong, and probably reflects a distinctive kind of worship practice.

From about 1200 pointed arches appear in church buildings, as part of a Europe-wide phenomenon. The larger religious foundations (abbeys and cathedrals) adopted this style – the Gothic – with vigour, creating great churches which became important centres of pilgrimage, especially for people conscious of guilt for their actions, who wanted formal forgiveness by priests. From the 14th century, with the cost of founding abbeys no longer affordable, noble families established friaries in towns and 'collegiate' churches, staffed by groups of priests who were endowed to say Masses for the souls of dead members of the noble families. In the towns (burghs) which had been founded as part of feudalization the burghers (merchants and tradesmen) also established collegiate churches.

The buildings and parts of buildings included in this section range from reasonably complete churches still in use through parts of large churches reduced in scale after the Reformation to fragments such as doorways, apses and chancel arches which survived post-Reformation rebuilding of churches to suit changes in worship practice and to accommodate larger congregations. The survival of so many buildings and parts of buildings speaks of economical re-use, but also, I believe, of a strong residual affection for the 'Old Religion' among many Scots.

The Reformation of the Church in Scotland was formalised in 1560 by an Act of the Scottish Parliament, but had been stirring for some time before that as part of a western European rejection of aspects of the Roman Catholic Church. Henry VIII in England had 'reformed' the Church in England, making himself Head of the Church, closing down all religious houses (monasteries, friaries and so on) and seizing their property, allocating their land to favoured nobles. In Scotland the reformers rejected the idea that the monarch should be head of the Church, regarding Christ as head of the Church. Religious houses were closed, but the monks, friars and nuns were allowed to continue to live in them to the ends of their natural lives. The saying of the Mass was prohibited, as was the praying for the souls of the dead. The focus of worship in church buildings moved from the altar to the pulpit, from which the Word of God was read and preached in the languages of the people. It was important that all those who attended worship should be able to hear what was being said. An important practical move was the prohibition of burials within churches, very desirable for hygienic reasons. Both the changes in worship practice and the end of church burial had considerable repercussions for the layout of churches, as was the expectation that parishioners would attend divine worship. Existing churches were modified, often with the abandonment of parts of larger buildings, or their division to accommodate more than one congregation. Interiors were modified to place due emphasis on the central role of the pulpit, and on the need for parishioners to hear what was being read and preached. Communion was celebrated rarely, and for the administration of the Sacrament tables were set out either in front of the pulpit, or in a separate part of the church, the Communion aisle. Baptism had to be administered in front of the congregation, and baptismal bowls were often bracketed from pulpits.

After 1603, when James VI became monarch of the United Kingdom of England and Scotland, he began to try to assimilate the Church of Scotland to the Church of England, which had retained many pre-Reformation beliefs and worship practices. In 1611 he was able to reintroduce bishops in the Church of Scotland (probably on a Danish-Lutheran model – his wife was Danish). However he wisely refrained from further integration. His original heir, Prince Henry, having died, James was succeeded by Charles

I, who inherited none of his father's discretion, and accepted Archbishop Laud's advice to integrate the Church of Scotland with the Church of England. Laud had previously tightened up the administration of the latter. Charles I's intention was bitterly resented by the Scots, who drew up the National Covenant with the objective of retaining Scots Reformed worship practices, rather than adopting the formalised rituals of the Church of England. This began a period of more than twenty years of religious and civil unrest, during which Charles was executed, bishops were abolished, and for a time Oliver Cromwell ruled Scotland, England and Ireland. During that period two new denominations were introduced from England, the Congregationalists and the Baptists.

Charles II was crowned King of Scots in 1651, and was restored as monarch of the United Kingdom in 1660. He speedily restored bishops, and began a programme of forcing everyone to adhere to the State version of Christianity. Worship practice within the Established Church, however, seems to have reverted to that of James VI's period of episcopacy. The Covenanters, who adhered both to the National Covenant of 1638 and to the more radical Solemn League and Covenant of 1643, rejected Charles II's moves, and as a result were persecuted by the Government forces both of Charles and of his brother and successor James VII. James was a Roman Catholic, and was thought to be planning to restore Roman Catholicism as the State religion. As there were similar fears in England, William, Prince of Orange and Stadtholder of the Netherlands, and his wife Mary were invited to take over the throne of the United Kingdom, which they did in 1689. William brought over with him William Carstares, who had fled from Scotland during the reign of Charles II on account of his Reformed religious beliefs.

On the advice of Carstares, William, in the Revolution Settlement of 1690, abolished episcopacy in Scotland, replacing it by a strict form of Calvinist Presbyterianism. This was accepted by most Scots, and is still the basis of the polity of the Church of Scotland and of the Free and other Reformed churches in Scotland. Two relatively small groups, however, did not accept the Carstares reorganisation. Some Episcopalians, despite persecution, continued their pre-1690 beliefs and worship practices, and refused to accept William and Mary as their lawful monarchs, believing that according to the Divine Right of Kings the Stuarts were their rightful kings. They went on, for that reason, after our period, to support the Jacobite risings of 1715 and 1745. The other group which 'stayed out' were the Covenanters, who rejected any State involvement in the affairs of the Church, and who formed a body known at the time as the Cameronians, after one of their leaders, Richard Cameron, who had been killed in 1680 at Airds Moss, near Cumnock during the conflict with the forces of Charles II. In 1743 this body became the Reformed Presbyterian Presbytery.

Because many of the churches which were inherited at the Reformation were capable of being adapted for Reformed worship, and because of the religious and civil uncertainties of the 17th century, there was little new church building between 1560 and 1700. A notable feature of many churches was, however, the construction of burial aisles, as a consequence of the prohibition of burials in churches, as previously mentioned. The few new churches of this period which have survived are generally well-designed, and they embody the changes in worship practice referred to earlier in this introduction.

Note: **D** after a caption means demolished: **A** means adapted to other uses or disused

Kirkmadrine, Wigtownshire
This little church in the Rhinns of Wigtownshire is on the site of a very early Christian graveyard, and now displays some of the 5th century grave-markers found there. There may well have been a church here at that time, but no above-ground evidence of one survives.

The Churchyard Stone, Aberlemno, Angus
Here there was obviously a Pictish sacred site, with three 'symbol stones'. This one, in the churchyard, probably dates from the 8th century, and is one of the finest of its type. The cross is decorated by abstract patterns (interlace, key-pattern and spirals), while round it, and on the back, are stylised representations of men and animals. Stones like this probably acted as focal points for worship before churches were built.

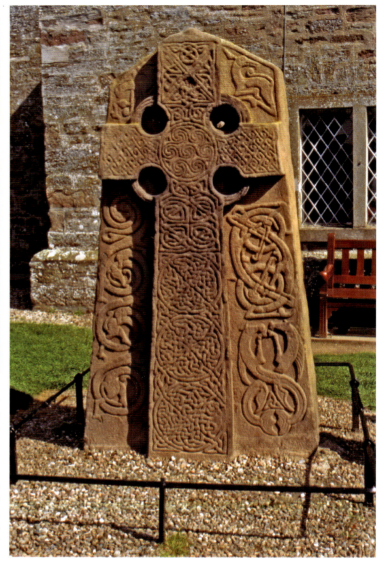

The Round Tower, Brechin, Angus

Round towers like this are characteristic of Irish churches of the 11th century. This one, now linked to Brechin Cathedral, is the only complete example in Scotland; there are others at Abernethy, Perthshire, and on the island of Egilsay, Orkney. The entrance is at first-floor level, and the tower was probably a refuge. The conical cap is later.

The Round Tower, Brechin, Angus

The entrance to the tower, with its delicately-carved surround. The representation of the crucified Christ at the head is an unusual survivor from the destruction of pre-Reformation symbols after that event.

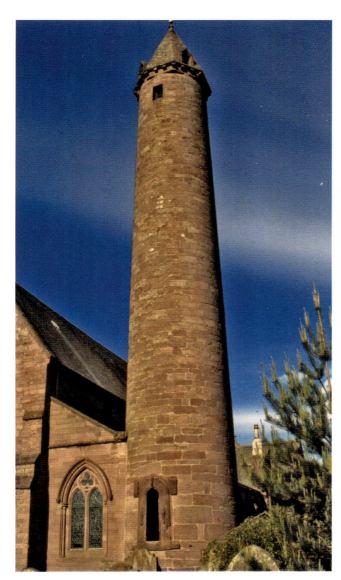

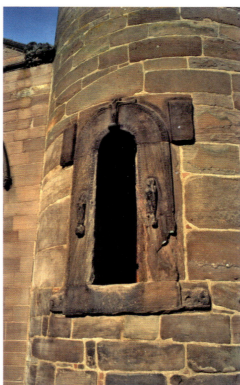

The Netherton Cross, Hamilton Old Parish Church, Lanarkshire

Probably carved in the 11th century, this cross was originally on the North Haugh, Hamilton, and was placed on its present site in 1926. It is a much less accomplished piece of carving than the Aberlemno Stone, but probably fulfilled the same role. By its very simplicity and vigour it is a moving and inspiring piece of work

Restenneth Priory, Angus

This was the church of a priory apparently founded in the 11th of 12th century. The tower probably dates from that period, and the choir, to the right was rebuilt in the 13th century. The steeple was added in about 1500. In common with all other religious houses, the priory was disbanded after the Reformation in 1560.

The Round Church, Orphir, Orkney

A handful of 12th century circular churches survive in Britain. This is the only Scottish example, and is now in the care of Scottish Ministers. These circular churches are supposed to have been modelled on the Church of the Holy Sepulchre in Jerusalem.

St Rule's Tower, St Andrews, Fife

This is the tallest and most complete of a group of 12th century Scottish square-plan towers. It abuts the chancel of a tiny church designed to house the relics of a saint. The scale of this tower suggests that it was intended to be a sea-mark for pilgrims coming to St Andrews by ship.

Stobo Parish Church, Peebles-shire

Set in lovely rolling Borders countryside, Stobo is a well-preserved example of a small 12th century parish church, with a short square tower with a saddle-back roof. It was built in about 1128, and partly restored in 1813 by John Lessels. The pointed windows date from that restoration.

Dalmeny Parish Church, West Lothian
This is the most complete 12th century church in Scotland, dating from about 1130. Like churches of this period in eastern England and in parts of western Europe it has three compartments, the eastmost being a semicircular apse. The tower on the left is a 20th century replacement for the long-vanished original

Dalmeny Parish Church, West Lothian
This view shows the south doorway of the church, with Romanesque doorhead and windows. These are characteristic of the period, as are the interlaced 'blind' arches above the doorway and the grotesque carvings round the door-head and above the blind arches (*see above*).

10

Dunblane Cathedral, Perthshire

Though most of this cathedral was built during the 13th century, the lower part of the tower (darker in this view) dates from the early 12th century, and was probably originally free-standing.

St Fillan's Parish Church, Aberdour, Fife

This little church, close to Aberdour Castle, conveys a sense of antiquity, but its early origin (c1140) cannot be seen from the exterior, except in the chancel on the right. The south aisle and porch were added in about 1500, and the belfry is post-Reformation. This church was unroofed in about 1890, but was sympathetically restored in 1926 by W Williamson.

Monymusk Parish Church, Aberdeenshire

This village church in rural Aberdeenshire was originally constructed in the second quarter of the 12th century. The arrangement of nave windows seen here dates from 1822. The church was again altered in 1892, when the tower was cut down and given a castellated top, and the nave altered to conform to the fashion of the time. The church was restored in 1929-32 by A Marshall Mackenzie of Aberdeen, when original features of the 12th century church were exposed.

Dunfermline Abbey Church, Fife

The great abbey of Dunfermline was founded in the 11th century, but the abbey church was rebuilt on a much grander scale in 1150. After the Reformation the magnificent Romanesque nave was retained as the parish church of the burgh. It has survived as the finest piece of Romanesque architecture in mainland Scotland, and is now in the care of Scottish Ministers. This is the west doorway, with grotesque sculpture round its head.

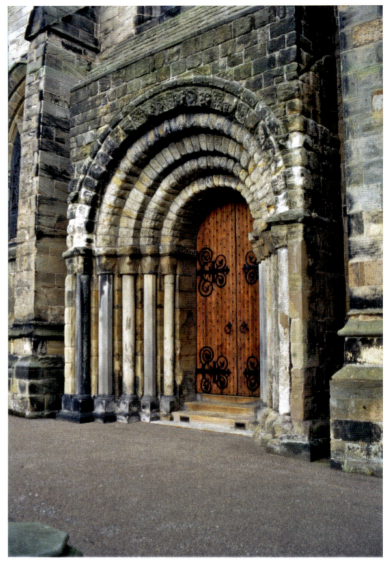

St Baldred's Church, Tyninghame, East Lothian

These are the skeletal remains of a fine mid-12th century Romanesque church like that at Dalmeny. Enough survives to show that the design of the building was of the highest standard. In 1761 the village it served was cleared, and it is now in the grounds of Tyninghame House.

Kelso Abbey, Roxburghshire

The Border abbey of Kelso was a 12th century foundation, and in its day was one of the largest Romanesque churches in Scotland. Most of it was demolished after the Reformation, but part of the west end, as seen here, survives to suggest the scale of the complete building.

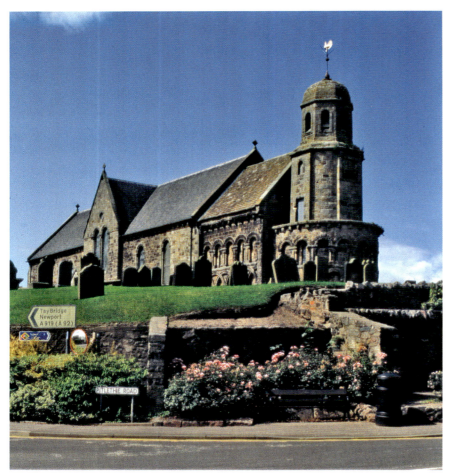

The church of St Athernase, Leuchars, Fife
What we see here has had a complex history. The choir and apsidal chancel are of the mid-12th century, but the bell-tower was not added until about 1700. In 1857-58 the nave (left) was added to designs by John Milne, who also restored the Romanesque fabric. The church sits on a mound in the centre of the village, which may have been a pre-Christian sacred site.

Symington Parish Church, Ayrshire
This is the most complete Romanesque church in the west of Scotland. It was built in about 1160 on a rectangular plan, and was extended by adding a wing on the north side (right in this view) in 1797. It was not until restoration was started in 1919, by Peter Macgregor Chalmers, that the extent of the survival of 12th century work was revealed.

Birnie Parish Church, Moray

This is another small Romanesque 12th century church, probably dating from the 1120s, and therefore one of the oldest surviving in Scotland. It has since been altered on several occasions. The round-headed windows in this view date from a restoration in about 1970 by John Wright of Elgin.

Lamington Parish Church, Lanarkshire

The first church on this site was built in the 12th century, and this doorway dates from that time. The rest of the church was rebuilt in 1721 and subsequently altered in 1828 and again in about 1880, when the village was improved by the landowner.　　　　**A**

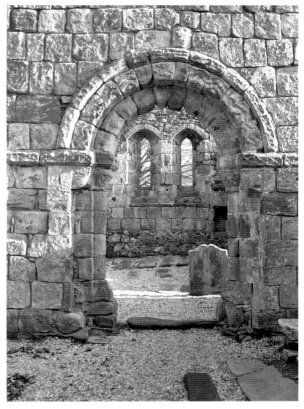

St Blane's Chapel, Isle of Bute

St Blane was a 6th century Christian missionary, and worship here may date back to that time. The remains of this little chapel date in part from the 12th century, as suggested by the semicircular chancel arch in this view. The lancet windows date from the 14th or 15th century. The chapel and the walls of its associated graveyard were conserved and partly rebuilt in about 1895 for the Third Marquess of Bute by Robert Weir Schultz.

The Cathedral of St Magnus, Kirkwall, Orkney

Unquestionably the finest Romanesque church in Scotland, it was planned as a memorial to St Magnus the Martyr, murdered by his brother on the island of Egilsay. Construction took from the 12th century to the early 16th century. The nave, with massive cylindrical piers, is like a miniature version of that at Durham Cathedral.

Markinch Parish Church, Fife

Like Leuchars this church is on a mound in the centre of the town. It was built in the 12th century, and the tower is recognisably of that period. The body of the church was rebuilt in 1786, using much of the original masonry. The Georgian spire was added in 1807. Recent investigations have revealed substantial remains of the mediaeval building.

Kirkliston Parish Church, West Lothian

At first sight this does not look like a 12th century building, but much of the fabric is of that period. The south doorway, in the centre of this view, dates from the late 12th century. The building was altered in 1865 and again in 1883.

Buittle Parish Church, Kirkcudbrightshire

This roofless building was built from the 12th century to the 13th century as a rural parish church, and rebuilt in 1743-45. The pointed chancel arch and the windows in the east end, seen in this view, date from the later 13th century.

Dundrennan Abbey, Kirkcudbrightshire

During the mid-12th century abbeys were established in many parts of Scotland, with the encouragement of the Kings of Scots, notably David I. Dundrennan was founded, possibly in 1148, by St Malachy, Bishop of Armagh, for Cistercian monks. The church was probably completed by about 1200. Much of the abbey was demolished after the Reformation in 1560, but the east end (seen here) was used as the parish church until 1742. The simple Gothic architecture is typical of Cistercian work. The ruins have been in State care since 1841.

St Mary's Parish Church, Auchindoir, Aberdeenshire

This little rural parish church was built in about 1200, the date of this fine late-Romanesque south door. The building was remodelled in the early 16th century, when a fine Sacrament House was added. After the Reformation it was remodelled as a Protestant parish church in 1638, and enlarged in 1664. It was replaced in 1811 by a new parish church, and then unroofed.

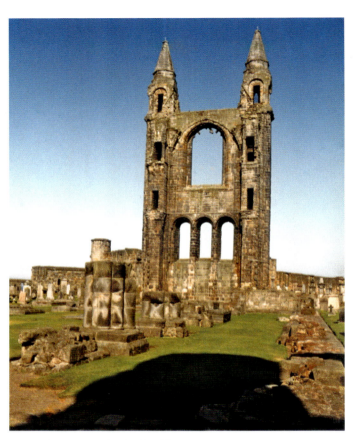

St Andrews Cathedral, Fife

St Andrews Cathedral was the largest pre-Reformation church in Scotland, and a noted place of pilgrimage to the relics of St Andrew, patron saint of Scotland. Most of the building was used as a quarry after the Reformation. The most substantial survival is the central part of the east end, which was built in about 1200, at the time of the transition from Romanesque to Gothic architecture, hence the mixture of round-headed and pointed arches.

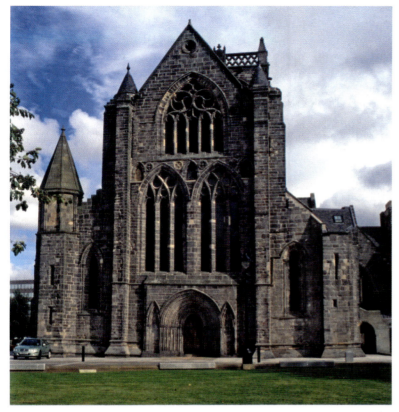

Paisley Abbey, Renfrewshire

The abbey in Paisley has a long and complex history. It was founded on this site as a priory in 1167 by Walter FitzAlan, High Steward of Scotland, with monks from Much Wenlock in Shropshire, his home county. One doorway survives from soon after its foundation. The west door of the nave, shown here, was built in the mid-13th century, and the rest of the nave constructed in the 15th century. The nave survived the Reformation as the parish church of Paisley. It was restored in 1859-62 by James Salmon, Senior, of Glasgow. Most of the rest of the church dates from the late-19th and early 20th century.

St Serf's Parish Church, Dunning, Perthshire

Rather like Markinch, the tower of this church is the least-altered part of a church, in this case built in about 1200. The body of the church was remodelled in the late 17th century, and again in 1808-11 by Alexander Bowie and John Frazer, though a substantial amount of original fabric was retained. The church, which is in State care, now houses the Dupplin Cross, a remarkable early-9th century carved stone. **A**

Kilwinning Abbey, Ayrshire

This abbey was founded in 1162-1189 by Richard de Morville. The abbey church was used as the parish church of the town until 1775, when a new church (in the background in this photo) was built. The most substantial survival from the original abbey church is the gable of the south transept, a good example of 13th century Gothic.

Kilmory Knap Chapel, Argyll

The county of Argyll is much broken up by sea lochs, and was never densely settled. Ruined mediaeval chapels can be found all over the area, usually single-chamber churches. This one dates from the early 13th century, and survived as a parish church for a remote part of the county. In 1934 it was consolidated, and a concealed glazed roof installed to provide a shelter for a remarkable collection of mediaeval carved stones. It is in State care.

A

Prestonkirk, East Linton, East Lothian

This parish church has a 13th century choir, in the simple Gothic of the period. The body of the church, on the left, was rebuilt in 1770. This is another church on a mound, like Leuchars and Markinch.

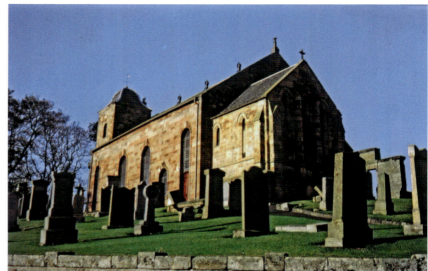

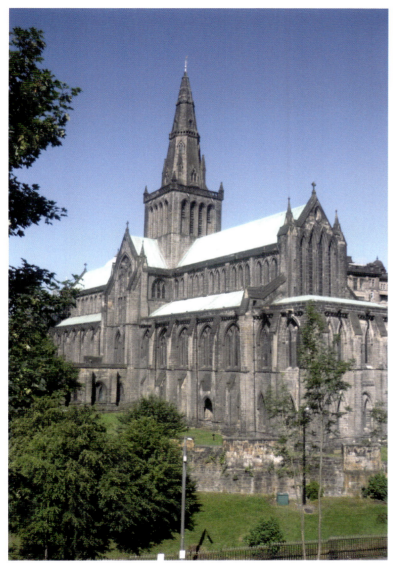

The Cathedral Church of St Kentigern (St Mungo), Glasgow

In the 12th century construction of a Romanesque church on this site, traditionally associated with St Kentigern, was begun. Within a very few years this was dismantled, and the building of the church in this view commenced. Its construction was largely completed during the 13th century, but the tower and spire were not added until the first half of the 15th century. It survived the Reformation and was used as a church for three parishes at different times. It has been restored on several occasions, but its fabric is largely original. It is in State care.

The Maison Dieu Chapel, Brechin, Angus

This fragment is all that is left of an almshouse founded in the mid-13th century by Sir William de Brechin, lord of Brechin. It is in State care.

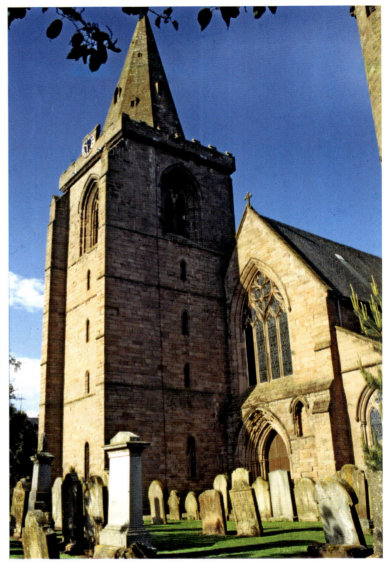

Brechin Cathedral, Angus

The round tower of Brechin has already been noted. The cathedral was built between the 13th and the 15th century adjacent to the tower. The nave and tower survived the Reformation as the parish church of the town, but the nave was much altered. In the early 20th century the church (including the choir, roofless for many years) was restored by the Glasgow architect John Honeyman.

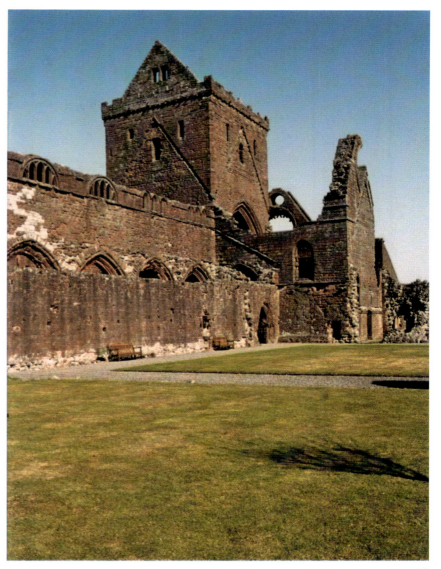

Sweetheart Abbey, New Abbey, Kirkcudbrightshire
This was the last pre-Reformation abbey established in Scotland and was founded in 1273 by Dervorgilla, widow of John Balliol, in memory of her husband. After the Reformation the abbey church survived largely as a ruin, though part of it housed the parish church of the village until 1877. In 1779 the rest of the roofless church was saved by a group of local landowners from use as a quarry. It has been in State care since 1928.

St Ternan's Parish Church, Arbuthnott, Kincardineshire

The earliest part of this lovely little rural church is the nave, on the left, built in the 13th century. On the right is a chapel added in 1506. The building was damaged by fire in 1889, and was restored by the Aberdeen architect A Marshall Mackenzie. It was again restored in 1952-53.

St Monan's Parish Church, Fife

This wonderful parish church sits on a cliff to the west of the town it serves, on the shores of the Firth of Forth. It was built between 1362 and 1370 by David II, and consists of the choir (retained as the parish church after the Reformation) and transepts; a nave was not built. The church has been sensitively restored on several occasions, notably by William Burn in 1826-28, who reroofed the transepts.

Temple Old Parish Church, Midlothian

This church was founded in the mid-14th century by the Knights Templar of the Order of St John. The building is largely of that period, but the belfry was added in the 17th or 18th century, when the building was being used as the parish church of a rural area.

Melrose Abbey, Roxburghshire

Melrose Abbey was founded in about 1136 by David I as part of his programme of reforming religious practice in Lowland Scotland. This Cistercian community was ravaged in several English attacks, notably in 1385 and 1544-45. Much of the abbey church was rebuilt in the early 15th century, including the south transept, seen in this view. After the Reformation the choir of the church (left in this view) was altered for Protestant worship in 1621, and the belfry on the transept gable was added at that time.

Cupar Old and St Michael of Tarvit Parish Church, Fife

The tower and a short section of an arcade are all that is left of a church built in 1415. The tower in this view is one of a series of such structures built in east Fife at that time. The upper part of the tower and the steeple were added in 1620. Note that the tower is wider than it is deep.

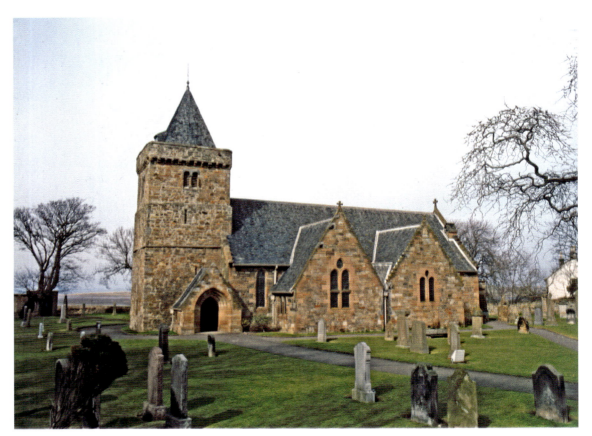

Aberlady Parish Church, East Lothian

The only surviving mediaeval part of this delightful church is the 15th century tower. On the north side of the body of the church are two early post-Reformation burial aisles, which were replicated on the south side (seen here) when the church was remodelled in 1886 by William Young.

Dunkeld Cathedral, Perthshire

Dunkeld Cathedral sits beside the River Tay next to the little town of the same name. The church was built during the 15th century. After the Reformation the choir was retained as the parish church, which function it still performs, though much altered. The nave and tower, seen in this view, though unroofed, are remarkably well-preserved.

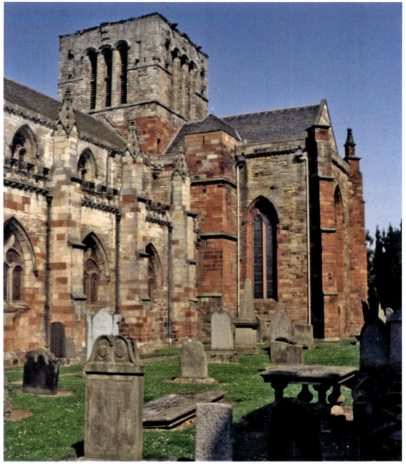

St Mary's Parish Church, Haddington, East Lothian

Built in the 15th century as one of Scotland's largest collegiate churches, the nave was unroofed after the Reformation, while the choir became the parish church. The aisle walls, on the left in this view, were raised in 1811 by James Burn and Archibald Elliot. The roof of the nave was restored in 1971-73 by Ian G Lindsay and Partners.

Crichton Parish Church, Midlothian

Close to the striking Crichton Castle, this pleasingly simple little collegiate church was built in about 1450. The nave may never have been built. After closure as a parish church some years ago it was taken over by a Trust, which uses the building for community events. **A**

St John's Parish Church, Perth

St John's is another large 15th century collegiate burgh church, its scale and sophistication evidence of the prosperity of the major Scottish burghs at that time. It had a complex post-Reformation history, and was restored between 1923 and 1926 to designs by Sir Robert Lorimer, as a memorial to the war dead of the city. The lead-covered wooden steeple is a notable feature.

The Chapel of St Salvator's College, University of St Andrews, Fife

St Salvator's College of the University of St Andrews (founded in 1413) was established in 1450 by Bishop James Kennedy, and this chapel was built between 1450 and 1460 to serve the college. Its splendid tower and steeple were probably intended as land and sea marks. It contains the extraordinary tomb of Bishop Kennedy.

Torphichen Preceptory, West Lothian

This church was founded in the 12th century as the Scottish headquarters of the Knights Hospitallers of the Order of St John. The only surviving part consists of the crossing and transepts of the church as rebuilt in the 15th century. Their unusual height is due to the existence of rooms above the church proper. The building is now in State care.   A

St Michael's Parish Church, Linlithgow, West Lothian

This is probably the finest 15th century burgh church in Scotland and sits next to Linlithgow Palace. It was restored in 1812, and again in 1894-96, by Honeyman and Keppie. Originally the tower had a crown steeple, like that of St Giles, Edinburgh, but this was taken down in the 19th century. The present aluminium-clad steeple was installed in the 1960s to a design by Geoffrey Clarke.

St Bride's Parish Church, Bothwell, Lanarkshire

St Bride's collegiate church was founded in 1398 by Archibald, 3rd Earl of Douglas, on the basis of an existing parish church. All that is left of the mediaeval church is the 15th century choir in this view, vaulted with a stone-slabbed roof. After the Reformation it was walled off as a burial aisle for the Douglas family. A new parish church was built on the site of the mediaeval nave in 1833, and the choir was integrated with that building in 1933. The choir has recently been restored by Tod and Taylor of Edinburgh.

St Mary's Collegiate Church, Dunglass, East Lothian

Another mid-15th century collegiate church, St Mary's is notable for its vaulted roofs with stone slabbing, a characteristic feature of the period. It was abandoned at the Reformation, and was later used as a barn, hence the rough doorway adapted from a window. It is now in State care.

Steeple of St Mary's Parish Church, Dundee

This enormous and magnificent tower was built on the west end of Dundee's large burgh church in the mid-late 15th century. The rest of the church was destroyed in 1548 by an English army. There are now three relatively-modern churches – the Steeple Church, St Peter's (the Mary Slessor Centre) and St Mary's – on the site of the ravaged mediaeval building. The steeple seems to have been designed to be capped by a crown steeple, like that of St Giles, Edinburgh.

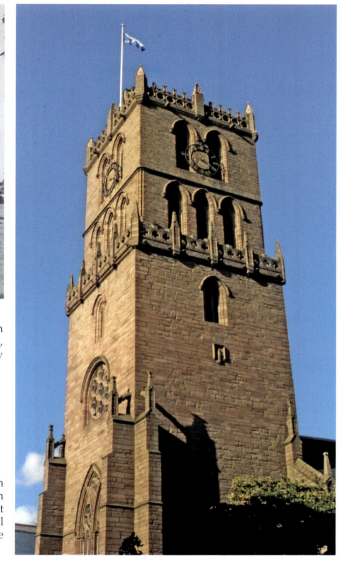

Kilbirnie Parish Church (The Auld Kirk), Ayrshire

This small-town church has an extraordinarily complex building history. The earliest part dates from the early 15th century, and the main body of the church from 1470. The tower (apart from the belfry, of 1854-55) was added in 1490. The Crawford aisle, on the right, was added in 1642. There is some remarkably fine woodwork of about 1700 in the interior.

The Strathmore Aisle, Glamis Parish Church, Angus

That this church was an early Christian site is shown by the presence of a Pictish cross in the grounds of the former manse, adjacent to the churchyard. The Strathmore Aisle, on the right, was built in about 1480 by Isabella Ogilvy, widow of Patrick Lyon, first Lord Glamis, in his memory. The church, on the left, was built in 1793.

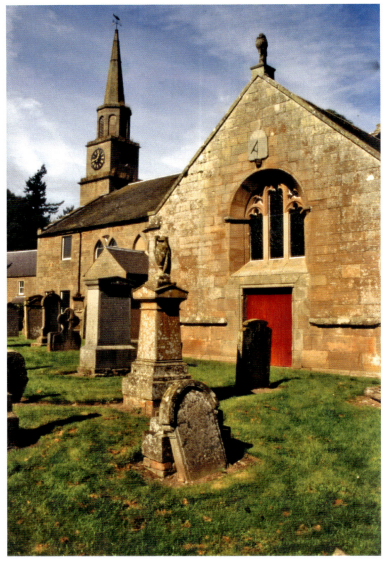

The High Kirk of St Giles (St Giles' Cathedral), Edinburgh

This was founded as the parish church of Edinburgh in the mid-12th century. The nave and transepts were built in the 14th century, the choir and steeple in the 15th century, and various chapels were added round this core. It was made into an Episcopal cathedral by Charles I and again by Charles II in the 17th century. After the restoration of Presbyterianism in 1689 it had a chequered history, being divided and used for various purposes. In 1829-33 it was re-clad by William Burn, and the west end, seen here, was later substantially altered. The crown steeple, however, remains as built in the late 15th century.

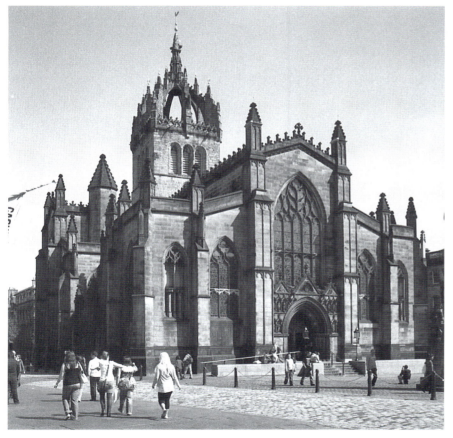

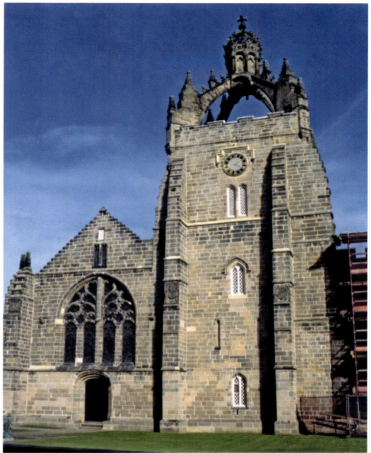

King's College Chapel, Old Aberdeen

King's College of the University of Aberdeen was established in 1495 by James IV, and the building of this chapel took place between about 1500 and 1509. The crown steeple was added in 1522, and was emblematic of the college's royal connection. As it retains some original internal fittings this is the most complete academic collegiate church in Scotland.

Kirkcaldy Old Parish Church, Fife

This was a mediaeval foundation, but the only remaining part surviving from that period is the tower, dating from about 1500. The belfry on top was added in the mid-18th century. The body of the church was rebuilt in 1806-08, to designs by James Elliot. **A**

Ladykirk, Berwickshire

This is one of the most remarkable late pre-Reformation churches in Scotland. It was built for James IV between about 1500 and 1507 on a hill overlooking the River Tweed, here the boundary between Scotland and England. It is entirely stone-vaulted, with stone slabbed roofs, like those at Dunglass and Bothwell. The chancel and transepts have polygonal ends, characteristic of Scots late Gothic churches. The bell-tower was added in 1741-43, and was probably designed by William Adam. **A**

Culross Abbey, Fife

Culross Abbey was founded in about 1215 as a Cistercian house by Malcolm, Earl of Fife. In about 1500 the nave of the abbey church was demolished, as no longer needed, and the tower seen here was built on top of the 'pulpitum', the stone partition which separated the nave from the choir. The top of the tower is later. The church was restored in 1905-06 by Sir Robert Rowand Anderson. In the foreground of the view on the right are remains of the residential buildings of the abbey, now in State care.

Straiton Parish Church, Ayrshire

This little church is the parish church of the Blairquhan Estate and its planned village. The aisle seen was added to a mediaeval church in about 1500 by the Kennedys of Blairquhan. The rest of the church was rebuilt in 1758, and the aisle was restored in 1889-91 by Kinross and Tarbolton. The tower (out of sight) was added by John Murdoch.

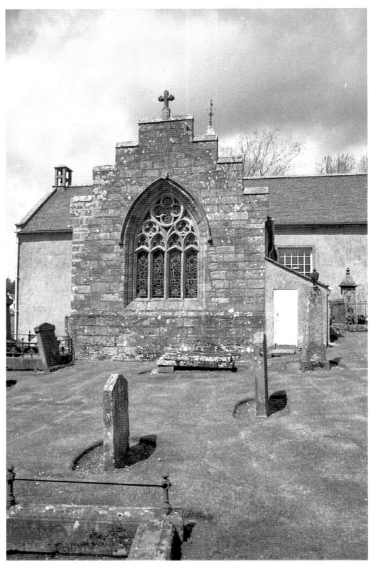

Castle Semple Collegiate Church, Lochwinnoch, Renfrewshire

In 1504-05 the local landowners, the Sempill family, built this little building as a private collegiate church. After the college of priests was disbanded at the Reformation the church was retained as a burial place for the family. It has unusual window tracery. Now in State care.

St Mary's Parish Church, Auchindoir, Aberdeenshire

This church featured earlier for its doorway of about 1200. As mentioned then the building was remodelled in the early 16th century, when this Sacrament House was inserted in the north wall of the building. This is one of a number of such features which survived the Reformation in north-east Scotland. They were used for keeping the 'Reserved Sacrament' (consecrated wafers) between Masses. This is one of the finest survivors. Now in State care.

The Church of the Holy Rude, Stirling.

This church may have been founded in the 12th century as a burgh church, but in its present form the nave dates from the mid-15th century, while the choir, seen here, was rebuilt from 1507 onward; at the same time a western tower was completed. After the Reformation the church was divided between two congregations, and was united after the First World War as a memorial to the war dead. The angled end so prominent is typical of Scots late Gothic design.

St Clement's Church, Rodel, Harris, Inverness-shire

Situated at the south-west end of Harris, this is the only large mediaeval church in the Western Isles. It was probably built for Alistair Crotach MacLeod of Dunvegan and Harris, as his tomb is in the church. It was abandoned after the Reformation, but was re-roofed in the 1780s and restored in 1873 by Alexander Ross. It is now in State care.   **A**

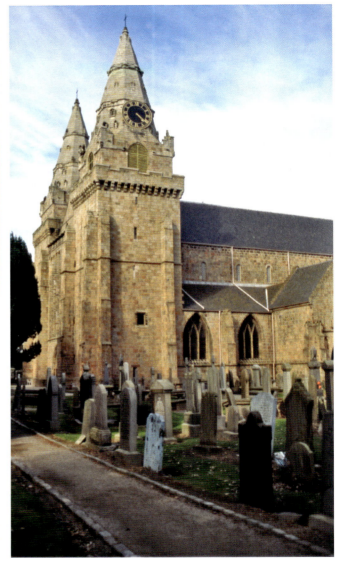

The Cathedral Church of St Mary and St Machar, Old Aberdeen

This large and sophisticated church has had a complex building history. After the Reformation the nave (1422-40) was retained as a parish church, but the rest was allowed to decay; the central tower fell in 1688. This view shows the west end of the church. The towers are of the 15th century, and the spires were added in about 1518-32, giving the nave a very commanding presence.

Dunnet Parish Church, Caithness

Dunnet is one of a small but important group of simple churches strung along the north coast of Caithness. The very plain body of the building may date from the 16th century; the tower was probably added in about 1700.

Deskford Old Parish Church, Banffshire

This long, low building contains a Sacrament House dated 1551, and much of the building may be of the pre-Reformation period. As seen here it shows signs of post-Reformation adaptation for Protestant worship. In State care.

The Hepburn Aisle, Oldhamstocks Parish Church, East Lothian

One of the acts of the Reformers after the Reformation was to end the practice of burial within church buildings. As a consequence landowning families began constructing 'burial aisles' adjacent to parish churches. This is a fine and early example, which with its Gothic tracery and stone-slab roof harks back to work of the earlier 16th century. It was constructed for the Hepburn family in 1581. Internally it is now part of the church.

Pittenweem Parish Church, Fife

Another post-Reformation practice was the addition of tolbooth towers to existing churches. This one at Pittenweem was built in about 1588. The church on the right is Victorian, but probably incorporates masonry from a mediaeval predecessor. The form of the steeple is very similar to that of a pre-Reformation Fife church.

St Quivox Parish Church, Auchincruive, Ayrshire

Built in 1595 for Richard Oswald of Auchincruive, this church has been altered on a number of occasions, notably in 1767, when an aisle was added on the north side. The basic form of what is seen in this view – a long, low building - is probably original.

Burntisland Parish Church, Fife

This was the first really important church built in Scotland after the Reformation, and it remains a building of the highest significance. It was built between 1592 and 1596 as a burgh church, on a central plan, with arches linking the corners of the building to piers supporting the tower and belfry. Over the years there have been alterations; the walls have been heightened, the wooden belfry replaced in stone, and galleries added internally, but the spirit of the original remains powerfully evident.

Dirleton Parish Church, East Lothian

Dirleton is an exceptional early 17th century church (c1615), long and low with a tower at one end. The top of the tower dates from 1836, and the projecting aisle from 1664, but otherwise the exterior of the building is little altered. The size of the church is an indication of the prosperity of East Lothian at that time.

The Charteris Aisle, Kinfauns Parish Church

Originally attached to a mediaeval church (part of the walls of which can be seen in the background in this view), this aisle (built in 1598) was retained when that church was replaced by a Victorian building. The simplicity of this building contrasts with the elaboration of the aisle at Oldhamstocks.

Greyfriars Parish Church, (Greyfriars Kirk) Edinburgh

Few churches have a more complex building history than Greyfriars, which was built to serve the growing south side of Edinburgh. Construction started in 1602, using stone from a convent at Sciennes. The east front, seen here, was completed in 1620. The window tracery was inserted in 1856-67 by David Cousin, an Edinburgh architect. See *The Buildings of Scotland: Edinburgh* for additional information about this fascinating building and its historic graveyard, in which the National Covenant was signed in 1638, an event of the most profound significance for the history of Britain.

The Munro Aisle, Kilmuir Easter, Ross and Cromarty

On the right in this view is another burial aisle originally attached to a pre-Reformation church. This one, for George Munro of Milntown, was constructed in 1616. The church to which it is now attached was built in 1797-98 and altered in 1903. The conical-roofed tower of the aisle is a unique feature.

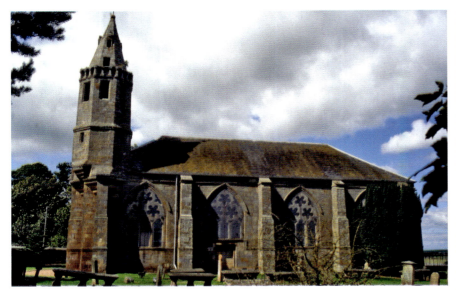

Dairsie Old Parish Church, Fife

Long disused for worship, this is a unique building. It was constructed in 1621 for the Episcopal Archbishop of St Andrews, John Spottiswoode, to introduce Anglican liturgical practice into Scotland. In this he failed, for the initiative was much resented, but the external expression of this can still be seen. The church was originally flat-roofed; the present one was installed in 1794. The building was restored in 1835-37.

Auchterhouse Parish Church, Angus

This is a little village church north of Dundee, and was originally built in about 1630. The body of the building was rebuilt in 1775, but the tower is probably the original 17th century one.

Pencaitland Parish Church, East Lothian

Another church with a complicated building history, Pencaitland was probably built in the late 16th century, but may incorporate some mediaeval fabric. The tower was added in 1631, and is unusually wider than it is deep.

Old Pitsligo Parish Church, near Rosehearty, Aberdeenshire

This roofless building was constructed in 1632 for Alexander Forbes of Pitsligo, on an equal-armed cross plan, typical of the periods of Episcopal church government in 17th century Scotland. The elaborate belfry, typical of Aberdeenshire at the time, is dated 1635. A wonderful 'laird's loft' was transferred to a successor building when it was constructed nearby in 1889-90.

St Congan's Old Parish Church, Turriff, Aberdeenshire
This church probably dates from the early 13th century, and the gable of the choir shown here was constructed in the 16th century. It is included here for its double belfry, dated 1635, installed after the church had been converted for Protestant worship.

The Tron Church, Glasgow
The original Tron Church in Trongate was built to complement the Cathedral as a place of worship for the city of Glasgow. The body of the church was destroyed by fire in the late 18th century and replaced by a plain building, now a theatre. This tower was built from about 1592, with the steeple added in 1630-34, at a time when the city was notably prosperous. The design of the steeple is based on that of the Cathedral spire.

Kirkmaiden Parish Church, Wigtownshire

Kirkmaiden is the furthest south-west parish in Scotland, and this little church (constructed from 1638) is one of the oldest surviving post-Reformation churches, in an area associated with the earliest Christianisation of the country. The belfry is a Victorian addition.

Fenwick Parish Church, Ayrshire

Fenwick is one of the best examples of a Greek (equal-armed) cross plan Scottish parish church. It was built in 1643, and restored, after a fire, in 1931-32 by Gabriel Steel. The belfry was rebuilt in 1864 by William Railton. The steep pitch of the roofs suggests that they were originally thatched.

Bowden Parish Church, Roxburghshire

In 1644 the Roxburghe family constructed a burial aisle, with a family loft above it, on the end of their parish church. This is the taller part of the building as seen here. In 1908-09 the church was remodelled by Peter MacGregor Chalmers, and the interior of this aisle was integrated into the body of the church. The fine family pew was moved to a new site.

Dalserf Parish Church, Lanarkshire

The first post-Reformation church here was built in 1655. It is not clear how much (if any) of the present building is of this period. It was rebuilt in 1721. The projecting wing and belfry were added in 1896 to create this unique profile.

Ardclach Bell Tower, Nairnshire

The parish church of Ardclach sits in a deep river valley below the site of this most moving little building, which housed the bell for the church. It was probably also used as a watch tower, as it was built at a time of political unrest. It is now in State care.

Burial aisle, Walston Parish Church, Lanarkshire

Walston is a rural parish in the south of Lanarkshire. This elegant 'Gothic Survival' burial aisle, with an 'intersecting-arc' window, was constructed in 1656, and the body of the small rectangular church was later added to the rear. **A**

Old St Peter's Parish Church, Thurso, Caithness

The oldest parts of this building were constructed in the 12th-13th century. It was remodelled in about 1500, and the aisle seen in this view was added in the 17th century. This example of 'intersecting-arc' tracery, characteristic of the period, is the finest in Scotland. The church was unroofed when a new St Peter's was built in the town centre in 1830-32, but the ruin is still in good condition.

St Talorgan's Parish Church, Fordyce, Banffshire

The mediaeval parish church of this little village continued in use after the Reformation. In 1661 its tower was heightened, and a new bellcote added, as seen here. This is another example of the characteristic 17th century belfries of north-east Scotland.

The Archerfield Aisle, Dirleton Parish Church, East Lothian

The early 17th century parish church here has already been illustrated. To its south side was added in 1664 this striking burial aisle in mixed Classical and Gothic styles, a very early example of Classical influence on Scottish church building. It now serves as the main entrance to the church.

Lauder Parish Church, Berwickshire
Lauder was laid out by the Duke of Lauderdale, whose Thirlestane Castle residence is nearby. The parish church was built on a Greek cross plan in 1673-74, to a design by Sir William Bruce. It was restored in 1973 by Neil Jack of Miller and Black.

Greenlaw Parish Church, Berwickshire
Greenlaw was for a time the county town of Berwickshire. The parish church (on the right in this view) was built in 1675. At a little distance from it the tolbooth tower was built in 1696, and the two were linked in 1712 to form an impressive combination.

Alloa Old Parish Church (St Mungo's), Clackmannanshire

Set in its graveyard, this is the tower and west gable of a church built in 1681-83 to serve the town of Alloa. The refined detail of the masonry of the upper part of the tower is characteristic of late 17th century Scots building of the better class. The design of the slated steeple is peculiar to the local area. The statue in the niche in the gable is said to represent St Mungo.

Gateway, Rutherglen Old Parish Church, Lanarkshire

There has been a church on this site since the 12th century, which was enlarged and altered on many occasions. In 1662-63 this Renaissance gateway was built to give access to the church and churchyard. Beyond the gate on the right can be seen one of a pair of 'sentry boxes' which provided shelter for Elders collecting offerings for poor relief. The present church, in the background, was built in the late 19th century.

The Laigh Kirk (New Laigh Parish Church), Kilmarnock, Ayrshire

This is another 17th century tower, also very nicely detailed. The church to which it was attached was replaced in 1750, and again in 1802, to a design by Robert Johnstone. This tower is a striking landmark in the town.

The Canongate Kirk, Edinburgh

After the Reformation in 1560 the nave of the abbey church of Holyrood became the parish church of the burgh of Canongate, east of what was then the burgh of Edinburgh. When James VII ascended to the throne of the United Kingdom in 1685 he took over that building as a Roman Catholic Chapel Royal, and the Canongate Kirk was built as a replacement for the Episcopal congregation thus displaced. The new church was designed by James Smith, and was constructed between 1688 and 1691. Its plan reflects the pattern of Episcopal worship at the time. By the time it was completed Presbyterianism had replaced Episcopalianism as Scotland's official religion.

Gladsmuir Old Parish Church, East Lothian

This is the roofless ruin of one of the first parish churches built after 1689, when Presbyterianism was restored. It dates from 1695 and is on a T-plan, a very common arrangement in the 18th century. The 'birdcage' bellcote is typical of the time.

Pettinain Parish Church, Lanarkshire

This little church, dating from about 1694, with its rectangular windows, is typical of early post–1689 Church of Scotland churches. It was renovated in 1820, a likely date for the Classical bellcote. In the care of the Scottish Redundant Churches Trust.

New Monkland Parish Church, Lanarkshire

In 1698 a new church was constructed to serve the then-rural parish of New Monkland, near Airdrie. By 1776 the population of the area had grown to the point that a new, larger church was built to replace the body of the 1698 building, only the tower and steeple of which were retained. This little steeple can be seen, with its holes on its faces, as an ancestor of the Classical steeples of the mid-and late 18th century.